FIRST BIOGRAPHIES

George Washington

Cassie Mayer

Heinemann Library
Chicago, Illinois

Customer Service **888-454-2279**

Visit our Web site at **www.heinemannlibrary.com**

Photo research by Tracy Cummins and Heather Mauldin
Designed by Kimberly R. Miracle
Maps by Mapping Specialists, Ltd.
Printed and bound in China by Leo Paper Group

10 09
10 9 8 7 6 5 4 3 2

10 Digit ISBN: 1-4034-9972-1 (hc)   1-4034-9981-0 (pb)

Library of Congress Cataloging-in-Publication Data
Mayer, Cassie.
  George Washington / Cassie Mayer.
     p. cm. -- (First biographies)
  Includes bibliographical references and index.
  ISBN-13: 978-1-4034-9972-1 (hc)
  ISBN-13: 978-1-4034-9981-3 (pb)
  1. Washington, George, 1732-1799--Juvenile literature. 2. Presidents--United States--Biography--Juvenile literature. I. Title.
  E312.66.M325 2008
  973.4'1092--dc22
  [B]
                              2007010088

Acknowledgements
The author and publisher are grateful to the following for permission to reproduce copyright material: ©The Bridgeman Art Library International **pp. 6** (Free Library, Philadelphia, PA), **11** (Peter Newark American Pictures, Private Collection), **12** (Butler Institute of American Art), **19** (Peter Newark American Pictures, Private Collection), **21** (Peter Newark American Pictures, Private Collection); ©Corbis **pp. 7, 16** (Bettmann); ©Getty Images **pp. 4** (Stock Montage), **5, 18** (MPI), **22** (Stock Montage); ©The Granger Collection **pp. 14, 15**; ©Library of Congress Prints and Photographs Division **pp. 10, 13**; ©North Wind Picture Archives **pp. 17, 23**.

Cover image reproduced with permission of ©Getty Images (Stock Montage). Back cover image reproduced with permission of ©Library of Congress Prints and Photographs Division.

Contents

Introduction

George Washington was the first president of the United States. A president is the leader of a country.

Washington is called the "Father of His Country."

Early Life

Washington's home

Washington was born in 1732.
He lived in Virginia.

When Washington was a child, he
moved to a farm.

The Colonies

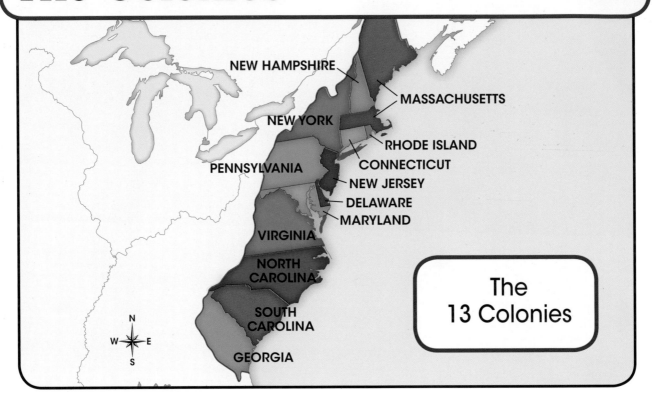

NEW HAMPSHIRE

MASSACHUSETTS

NEW YORK

RHODE ISLAND

CONNECTICUT

PENNSYLVANIA

NEW JERSEY

DELAWARE

MARYLAND

VIRGINIA

NORTH CAROLINA

SOUTH CAROLINA

GEORGIA

The 13 Colonies

The United States was not a country yet.
It was called the American colonies.

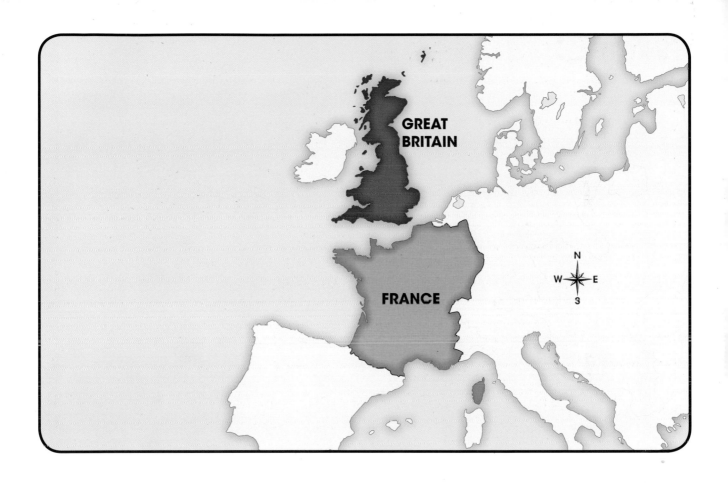

The colonies were led by Great Britain.
Some colonies were led by France.

War

Great Britain and France went to war in 1754. They fought over land in the colonies.

Washington led an army for Great Britain.
He was a great leader in the war.

Marriage

Washington left the war in 1758. He went home to marry Martha Dandridge Custis.

Washington became a leader in the colony of Virginia.

End of the War

The war between France and Great Britain ended in 1763. France gave its land in the colonies to Great Britain.

Great Britain became the leader of the colonies.

The American Revolution

In 1775, people in the colonies wanted to lead their own country.

They decided to go to war with Great Britain.

They chose Washington to be leader.

He was a great leader in the war.
He helped win against Great Britain.

A New Country

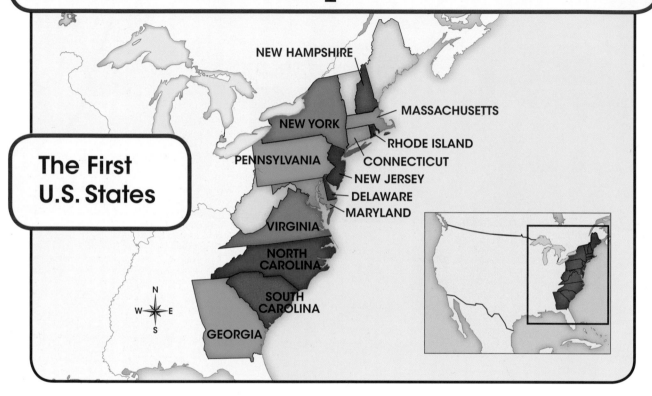

The First U.S. States

NEW HAMPSHIRE

MASSACHUSETTS

NEW YORK

RHODE ISLAND

PENNSYLVANIA

CONNECTICUT

NEW JERSEY

DELAWARE

MARYLAND

VIRGINIA

NORTH CAROLINA

SOUTH CAROLINA

GEORGIA

The colonies became a new country.
They became the United States of
America.

Washington became the first president of the United States in 1789.

Why We Remember Him

Washington was an important leader.
He helped lead the new country.

Picture Glossary

American Revolution war fought between the 13 colonies and Great Britain

colony an area of land that is ruled by another country

Timeline

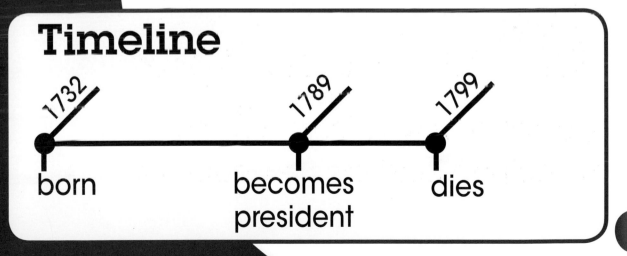

1732 born

1789 becomes president

1799 dies

Index

Note to Parents and Teachers

This series introduces prominent historical figures, focusing on the significant events of each person's life and their impact on American society. Illustrations and primary sources are used to enhance students' understanding of the text.

The text has been carefully chosen with the advice of a literacy expert to enable beginning readers success while reading independently or with moderate support. An expert in the field of early childhood social studies curriculum was consulted to provide interesting and appropriate content.

You can support children's nonfiction literacy skills by helping students use the table of contents, headings, picture glossary, and index.